G000068395

Girls Gotta Have Fun!

Other Books by Sue Buchanan

I'm Alive and the Doctor's Dead

Duh-Votions

Friends Through Thick and Thin
with Gloria Gaither, Peggy Benson, and Joy MacKenzie

Girls Gotta Have Fun!

101 Great Ideas for Celebrating Life
with Your Friends

Sue Buchanan

Illustrated by Don McLean

WOMEN OF FAITH℠

ZondervanPublishingHouse
Grand Rapids, Michigan

A Division of HarperCollinsPublishers

Girls Gotta Have Fun!
Copyright © 2000 by Sue Buchanan
Illustrations Copyright © 2000 by Don McLean

Requests for information should be addressed to:

 ZondervanPublishingHouse
Grand Rapids, Michigan 49530

Library of Congress Cataloging-in-Publication Data

Buchanan, Sue.
    Girls gotta have fun! : 101 great ideas for celebrating life with your firends / Sue Buchanan.
    p. cm.
    ISBN 0-310-22885-9 (hardcover)
    1. Female friendship Miscellanea. 2. Amusements Miscellanea. 3. Women—Conduct of life Miscellanea. 4. Female friendship—Religious aspects—Christianity. I. Title. II. Title: Girls got to have fun.
HQ1206.B797 1999
302.3'4'082—dc21
                                                    99-30108
                                                       CIP

This edition printed on acid-free paper.

All Scripture quotations, unless otherwise indicated, are taken from the *Holy Bible: New International Version*®. NIV®. Copyright © 1973, 1978, 1984 by International Bible Society. Used by permission of Zondervan Publishing House. All rights reserved.

All rights reserved. No part of this publication may be reproduced, stored in a retrieval system, or transmitted in any form or by any means—electronic, mechanical, photocopy, recording, or any other—except for brief quotations in printed reviews, without the prior permission of the publisher.

Published in association with the literary agency of Alive Communications, Inc., 1465 Kelly Johnson Blvd. #320, Colorado Springs, CO 80920.

Interior design by Laura Klynstra Blost

Printed in the United States of America

00 01 02 03 04 05 /❖ DC/ 10 9 8 7 6 5 4 3

WOMENOFFAITH℠

Women of Faith is partnering with Zondervan
Publishing House, Integrity Music, *Today's
Christian Woman* magazine, World Vision, and
Campus Crusade to offer conferences, publications,
worship music, and inspirational gifts that support
and encourage today's Christian women.

Since their beginning in January of 1996, the Women of
Faith conferences have enjoyed an enthusiastic welcome
by women across the country.

**Call 1-888-49-FAITH for the many conference
locations and dates available.**

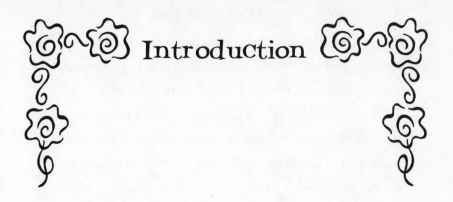

Introduction

Several years ago I wrote a book called *I'm Alive and the Doctor's Dead*. Its subtitle describes it best: *Surviving Cancer with Your Sense of Humor and Your Sexuality Intact*. Perhaps one of the reasons I survived (it's been seventeen years now!) was because of friends who came through with flying colors to surround me with joy and humor. When I speak in public about these unorthodox friends and the crazy things they did—and continue to do—to make my life joyous, I can count on the roar of the crowd.

One day a pastor's wife called me and announced she had pencil and paper in hand ready to take notes on things the women in her parish could do to nourish friendship. Another time my friends and I were remembering the crazy things we had done *to* and *for* each other over the years, and someone said to me, "You're a writer; write this stuff down."

The next day I pulled out a computer disk, stuck it in the slot, and wrote "Things—Friendship." *But surely people know this stuff,* I thought. *And most women are content with their lives as they are; those who need friends have them, and those who don't, don't care! Perhaps some people would like to have them, or* more *of them, as the case may be, but they simply aren't searching for added work—and it certainly takes work to be a friend.*

Nevertheless, I began to add to my file regularly. Simultaneously, I found myself listening to (and even eaves-dropping on!) other women, young and old, and with various life experiences, as they talked about their own friendships or lack of them. With my interest in the subject piqued, I found myself watching relationships at work, trying to tune in to the rhythms and body language of friendship.

My computer file kept growing and wouldn't stop. And I kept listening and talking with women, including those who don't have another minute in their day, and found they were hungry to know how to do it, or how to do it *better*—this art of friendship. Most of all, I found they loved sharing ideas for making friendship fun, whether the relationships were for a season or a lifetime.

The problem is, I can't bring my book to an end, even though my editor says I must. "A hundred and one! That's the absolute limit," she says. So now I'm wondering about the possibilities of an *unfinished* book. There was a symphony left unfinished, why not a book, for heaven's sake? If we left it open-ended, not only could I keep adding to it, but you could as well. You could send me your ideas by e-mail, fax, or even snail mail. What if our daughters caught the spirit? What if they took up the cause? What if after you and I have walked off into the sunset, they continued the process, and it went on and on through history, generation after generation, and it became kind of a *Guinness Unfinished Symphony of Friendship for All Time; World-Without-End-Amen* book? The title may be a little lengthy, and we would have to get permission from Guinness to use the name, but we have plenty of time to work on it.

"What's a computer?" our progenitors might someday ask as they read our thoughts. "What's a camera?" "A telephone?"

"What's Tupperware?" they'll say. " . . . Must be some mysterious delivery system used by our ancestors to exchange food gifts." "And a book mark? What's a book mark? What's a book?"

Perhaps when our great-great-great-grandchildren read that we sent each other flowers, they'll ask, "What's a flower?" Heaven forbid! But think of it! If we do this thing well and we all work together and the excitement builds and technology cooperates, the one question they *won't* be asking is "What's friendship?"

I hope you'll keep this book handy and refer to it often, not because it's the "final amen" on how to make new friendships and nourish old ones, but because it will trigger creativity in you. *Soon I'll be buying YOUR book!*

Another resource I highly recommend—and perhaps it *is* the final amen on friendship—is the Bible, the Word of God! It not only gives you guidelines for earthly friendships, but it will show you how to be friends with God. Without a doubt the most important Friend of all!

1

When a friend needs you, drop everything and go! "Everything" does *not* include a chocolate souffle or a bottle of hair color, and certainly not the baby!

2

Introduce each friend as "my best friend in the whole wide world," and when you call her on the phone say, "This is your very best friend in the whole wide world." You can have at least two dozen best friends in the whole wide world. More if you travel.

3

Give away something you love—children don't count!

4

Tune in! Find out what your friends love and act accordingly. If a friend loves cats, send her cards with cats on them. If she loves tea, give her a teacup or an assortment of exotic teas from around the world. How about a single tea bag attached to a helium-filled balloon? For a book lover, a gift certificate would be nice—or even a handful of bookmarks. For a gardener, give a watering can. If you have a friend whose hobby is nuclear science, you're on your own!

5

You can't brag too much about a friend. Think of yourself as her public relations agent. "That Lynn, she can do anything! She has more talent in one finger than most people have in their whole body!" "Marsha? There's nobody busier—being a state senator and all—but she'll drop everything and come when you need her. She's amazing!"

6

Rent a billboard to say "Happy Birthday," "Congratulations," or "I'm glad you finally got that kid raised and off to college." On second thought, in the case of the kid off to college, forget the billboard; send money!

7

G ive your friend a "maid for a day." If you're short of cash, dare I suggest *you* be the maid? When our friend Betsy was in the hospital, our church fellowship group pitched in and cleaned Betsy's house from top to bottom. We had a blast, and Betsy had a clean house when she came home.

8

Say, "What can I do?" and mean it. If your friend says, "Get lost!" don't hang around. Check back at intervals.

Say her new baby is cute, even if it's not.

Pray together. On your knees. Scripture says, "I tell you that if two of you on earth agree about anything you ask for, it will be done for you by my Father in heaven" (Matthew 18:19).

In January give each of your girlfriends a big wall calendar. (Insurance companies give them away free.) Use colorful markers and fill in dates with such things as "Throw away your husband's old socks day," "Read a mindless novel day," or "Take your friend Sue on a cruise week!" Write in your birthday with a black marker—circled and highlighted. Have a birthday three times a year—more if you think you can get away with it.

12

When you take food to someone in a Tupperware container, don't ask for the container back. *Let it go, for heaven's sake; it's only plastic!* Plastic containers should be circling the globe like satellites, stopping here and there to be emptied and refilled.

❧ 13 ❧

If a friend loses her job (or her husband loses his), send a humongous box of beans—dried beans, canned beans, soup beans, northern beans, pinto beans—all kinds of beans. Just for fun, wrap the box in plain brown paper and label it "explosives," "danger," and "handle at your own risk." If she loses her job again, don't do beans a second time.

14

When your friend is in a deep funk
Load her down with goos and gunk.
Give her lotsa bath stuff
(You can't get too much)
With a note saying "Happy tub dunk!"

Give squirt guns to
newlyweds.
Instructions won't
be necessary.
They'll know
exactly what
to do.

Get your gang together and sing through the hymn-book. A duet, a trio, or a quartet. If you have a lot of friends, make it a choir!

17

Give a gift subscription to a magazine. Choose one that fits the person. *Popular Mechanics* probably isn't ideal for your pastor's wife, and *Christian Parenting* might not be the magazine of choice for a lady wrestler.

18

My motto is "Friendship is a fifty-fifty proposition. I'll give you a fifty-cent card, and you give me a fifty-dollar blouse."
Wait! I'm joking! What I'm really saying here is the complete opposite: "Don't keep score!"
Remember:

It's a given that life isn't fair,
So don't ever try to compare
Your cars or your farm
Or the size of your barn,
'Cause you start and you end this
     life bare.

19

If you're flush with cash, give a cashmere sweater.

If you're short of cash, give a bookmark. Give it with the same aplomb you'd give a cashmere sweater.

21

If you're the recipient of a bookmark—or a cashmere sweater—accept either gift with the same degree of enthusiasm.

W hen your friend is busy, offer to take her car to be
washed. If the car is ordinary, return it to her immedi-
ately. If the car is a fancy-schmantzy sports car, take it for a spin
before you return it. Poke her in the ribs, wink, and say, "They
were lined up for miles at the car wash."

23

Send a "remember when" note. "Remember when we wore garter belts? White gloves?" Remember when "software" came wrapped in tissue paper and pink ribbon and made you blush?

24

Accept your friends only if they are perfect in every way. *Wrong!* Accept your friends unconditionally! And you'd better hope with all your heart and soul they do the same for you.

25

Give a gift certificate for a massage. A massage is like a mini-vacation.

❧ 26 ❧

If your friend is considering a face lift, give her a paper bag and tell her she has an option!

If you have a spat, send pick-up sticks and a note
to suggest you pick up where
you left off.

LET'S
PICK·UP
WHERE WE
LEFT OFF.

28

Keep a "stash" of children's books handy for your friends' children or grandchildren. (I have a big basket of books in the kitchen where they're easy to get to.) Choose books that are designed for "readability." Read and "perform" them with all the dynamics of a Broadway actor.

Jack'n'
Till

Form a good-natured conspiracy with your friends' children. Read *Weird Parents* (by Audrey Wood) aloud to them and giggle about *their* weird parents.

30

Don't be a whiny-piney. Don't say, "Why haven't I heard from you?" "Where have you been?" Accept the fact there's a reason and move on.

❧ 31 ❧

When your friend breaks up with her boyfriend, she needs a boost. She's probably worn her hair the way *he* liked it for heaven knows how long, so take her a stack of magazines and offer to help her choose a "new woman" hairdo.

If her boyfriend breaks up with *her*, have his photo enlarged and invite her to a game of darts.

33

Give children's books to your adult friends, books such as *If You Give a Moose a Muffin*, *Miss Fannie's Hat*, or *Miss Rumphius*. The message in a child's book often beats that of an adult book. Besides, who has the time to read *War and Peace* these days?

If you Give
a moose a
muffin

34

Speak the truth! Speak the truth in love, being careful of fragile feelings!

When you leave a message on her machine that doesn't need a response, *say so*. Say, "You don't have to call me back." It's a huge relief for a busy woman. Sometimes, just for the fun of it, leave a silly message. Use your Donald Duck voice. Make it short, for heaven's sake!

❧ 36 ❧

Buy your friend a Bible or New Testament to match her newest Sunday outfit. They have the most chic colors these days: purple, green, and teal blue to name a few.

Write letters. As electronic mail becomes more prevalent, letters sent *snail mail* will become treasures. Create them to be "keepers." Use lovely note paper and spray it with your own fragrance. Write in your most flowery penmanship. Begin with "My dearest friend."

38

Send e-mail. One sentence will do. "Hey, girlfriend. I'm praying for you today."

When you take pictures, ask for two copies and send the
extras to your friends. There's something wonderful
about receiving pictures a week or two after an event.

40

Do as my friend Evelyn does. She takes pictures and superimposes the faces of her friends on store-bought greeting cards. Nothing beats getting a picture of a sexy bikini-clad body with your own face on it. Most of the cards I get these days are saggy, shriveled up old ladies who look very much like me!

41

Celebrate the glorious seasons of the year with a friend!
Raucously rake leaves in awesome
   autumn.
Share snow shoveling in wondrous
   winter.
Take a walk in the spectacular spring.
Gather wildflowers on a splendid
   summer afternoon.

Or! . . . disregard the four previous suggestions and *shop* in the spring! Shop in the summer! Shop in the fall! And shop in the winter!

43

Share bulbs and cuttings from your gardens. That's *flower bulbs* not *light bulbs!*

44

If a friend is in the hospital, give her a feather boa to wear with her nightgown. She'll feel better in no time! (You can buy these where they sell children's dance costumes.)

❧ 45 ❧

Have a "Life is a Bowl of Cherries" party. Serve ice cream with cherry pie filling and whipped cream. Smear your noses and take pictures.

When a friend turns sixty-five and goes on Social Security, commend her for being the *absolute youngest person in the history of the world* to do so! Say you are sending her name to Ripley's *Believe It or Not!*

If your friend is single, include her in all the couples parties. Introduce her to a cute guy. (This is not a good idea if your friend is a nun!)

48

If, as in the case of my friend Peggy, your friend prefers to keep the memory of her deceased husband alive, let her! Speak of him as though he'll be right back. We say that on a cloudy day we see Peggy's husband, Bob, dancing on the clouds, and we quote him often: "As Bob Benson would say . . . !"

Scrapbook together. Occasionally, make color copies for your poor little pitiful mother back in Tennessee (or wherever!). My daughter Dana is hooked on the Creative Memories system and is a crop-till-you-drop kind of girl. After a family get-together I can count on receiving a color-copied page, or two, of interestingly captioned photos to display on my refrigerator.

❧ 50 ❧

If your friend is troubled, invite her to pray in a cathedral. Or a country church.

🌸 51 🌸

If you can afford it, pay for a cruise for you and a friend. If you can't afford a cruise, send her a card that says, "If I had the money … I'd take you on a cruise!"

52

Never say "I told you so!" or sing that obnoxious "Nana, Nana, Na, Na!" thing!

53

Don't ever make fun of her crazy shoes. Don't say, "If you fall off those platforms, you'll never get back on."

Gather up your friends and attend a women's conference. Stay in the same hotel room; the more the merrier! Bring an extra suitcase filled with junk food.

55

If your friend likes to cook, give her a funny apron. You'll find a good assortment in most kitchen stores; a flowered one, one with chili peppers, and I've even seen one that makes you look as though you're wearing a bikini. How about buying a plain white one and decorating it yourself? Grab a handful of colorful markers and write over and over: *Suubliiminaal meeessage: Inviiiiite Suuuuee [your name here instead of mine] ooover fooorrr dinnnnerrr.*

Invite your best friends for a flight in a hot air balloon. Important note: take a coffee can!

57

Listen! Listen again and again. Listen some more. Don't interrupt and don't offer suggestions; do not pass "Go" and do not collect two hundred dollars.

58

Be as genuinely enthusiastic about your friend's triumphs as you are sympathetic about her defeats.

59

When she complains that the tags in her dresses all say "L," say, "Oh, I've read about that! They've had a terrible time with those garment workers that don't speak English. The tags don't mean 'large.' They're really sevens! *They were sewn in upside down.*" Offer to help her reverse them.

If she gets a write-up in the newspaper, clip it, laminate it, and send it to her. This is not a good idea if she robbed a bank!

Sneak a decoration onto her Christmas tree. Attach a note that says, "When this noisy season is over, I'll treat you to a quiet lunch."

62

Don't be thin-skinned. There is nothing worse than a pouter. As my mother used to say "Get over it!"

❧ 63 ❧

Buy a kazoo (easily found in the toy department of your local drug store) and practice playing "Happy Birthday" (all you have to do is hum, for heaven's sake!). Call your friends on their birthdays and play it with panache. This is what my friend Mel does. In fact, she invented the idea.

Invite your friends to high tea. Wear hats and gloves and serve scones. Behave like proper ladies!

🌸 65 🌸

Have a slumber party, but heed this warning: Don't invite a masseuse. We tried that once, and everyone konked out before the junk food and gossip. What a waste!

Leave a magnet on her refrigerator. Perhaps a magnetic picture frame with a picture of the two of you.

67

Leave a funeral wreath in her yard on her birthday. Peggy and I have one—a very tacky one the color of PeptoBismal—that travels back and forth between our houses. We are never quite sure when it will show up again.

68

When your friend has an obvious weight loss, make her a bikini out of colorful gift-wrapping paper and ribbons.

If your friend has bad breath, say, "Want a mint?" If she says no, say, "Oh, yes you do!"

70

Encourage her when she redecorates, goes on a diet, takes tap dancing lessons, or begins a Bible study.

🌺 71 🌺

Videotape each other to create an oral history of your lives for posterity. Ask questions such as "What's your earliest memory?" "What did you love most about your mother and your father?" "When you were a child did you have a pet? Describe it." "Do you remember going to birthday parties?" "What did your house look like?" "Did you have a favorite out-fit?" "Do you remember going to Sunday school and church?" "What memory stands out about your first day of school?" "Who were your playmates and what did you do?" "What was your favorite vacation?"

72

Send postcards. Keep your eyes open for free ones from hotels, resorts, restaurants, or beverage companies. A friend sent me a wonderful postcard (a sausage company advertisement) with a pig on it when my picture was in the paper as the best-dressed person at the Swine Ball, a local fundraising event. Stash cards away as you find them to use as the opportunity arises. Don't apologize for the fact that it was free! You bought the stamp!

73

For a bridal shower, give your friend a recipe for a peanut butter sandwich. My friends Jan and Carlene gave me the following one forty years ago at my own shower. It's still the first recipe in my book:

Take two slices of white bread and one jar of peanut butter; set them in front of you. Place kitchen knife between first and second finger of one hand, dip knife in jar and collect a generous glob. Pick up slice of bread in your other hand and spread peanut butter on it using back-and-forth motion. Place second piece of bread on top of the first. Right side up. Chew heartily and swallow.

That "right side up" cracks me up!

Laugh with her about her old boyfriends. "Hey Deb, seen Baby Huey lately?" "How about Mr. Holy Grail? Good lookin' but *old enough to be your father!*"

75

Christmas gifts are expensive! Here's an alternative to spending money on gifts. Give the gift of "tradition." For instance, you could invite your friends and their children to the "First Annual Grinch Party." Watch *The Grinch That Stole Christmas*. Make the event interactive by saying the well-known tongue-twisters "tartinkers," "slew-slunkers," "who-wonkers," and "pan-tookas" along with the tape. Sing the songs. Talk back to the screen. "Oh, you rotten Grinch, you!" "Poor, poor Max!" "Not the roast beast!" "Poor little Cindy Lou Who!" Gasp at the appropriate time; sigh at the appropriate time. As the Grinch catches the spirit of Christmas, you can begin to cheer him on, ending with hand claps and "yeas!" Make a huge point of the fact that "Christmas Day will always be just as long as we have *we!*"

Rent a convertible. Drive with the top down through the middle of town singing oldies—*loudly!*

Spend the day at a flea market.
Set a price limit and stick to it.

78

If she compliments your earrings, take them off and give them to her. If they cost more than twenty dollars, tell her where you got them and offer to go with her to get some!

79

Watch for clever gifts to stash away till you need them:

Coming up with the perfect do-hickey
Isn't easy. In fact it's quite tricky
So stash away stuff
You can give off the cuff
When you have to come up with a
quicky.

80

Have an "Older Than Dirt Party." Serve "dirt cake":

Layer #1: Crush a package of chocolate sandwich cookies and smush into the bottom of a 9 x 13 pan.

Layer #2: Beat together an 8-oz. package of cream cheese, a half stick of margarine, and a cup of powdered sugar. Spread onto layer #1.

Layer #3: Mix together an 8-oz. whipped topping, 2 packages of vanilla pudding, and 3 and 1/2 cups of milk. Spread on top of layer #2.

Add some gummy worms, pushing them in with your fingers, till your dirt cake is *crawling*.

81

Speaking of cakes, try this one when the occasion—a birthday, a slumber party, or maybe a house warming—calls for something silly:

Buy four different flavored cake mixes and several different colors of frosting, including squirt cans. Follow the directions on the boxes for mixing the cakes, making one a sheet cake to use as a base and baking the others in different sized soup cans, fruit cans, cupcake tins, and tiny little muffin pans. No rules! Use what you have handy. After the cakes are cool, use the sheet cake as a base, and stack your cake together every-which-way using different colored frosting, sprinkles and candies.

82

A fun game: Give each person twelve pennies. Going around the circle, each person in turn says, "I am so old that . . ." The trick is to say something that is unique to you. For instance I might say I'm so old that I have mouse traps in my bread drawer. (True. We have problems with mice who come up through the backside of the drawer.) Since nobody else has mouse traps in their bread drawer, I would collect a penny from each person. The person with the most pennies at the end of the game wins.

83

For a fancy occasion, here's my favorite special-occasion baked Alaska. It will make you a best friend (and famous) overnight because it's spectacular. It's also easy! Here it is in just a few simple steps.

- Bake an off-the-shelf brownie mix. Use the directions for cake brownies, and bake it in one round pan.
- Cool, wrap, and freeze.
- As you are letting a half-gallon of ice cream (coffee or peppermint) soften, line a round, dome-shaped mixing bowl with plastic wrap or waxed paper. Pack the ice cream into the bowl and place it in the freezer.
- When you are ready to assemble your masterpiece, beat 5 egg whites stiff for meringue and add 6 to 8 tablespoons of sugar.

- Place the brownie cake on a small cookie sheet and turn the ice cream dome upside down on top of that (don't forget to peel off the plastic wrap).
- Once assembled, ice it with the egg-white mixture, being careful to cover the whole thing down to the cookie sheet. Using your knife or spatula, make peaks in the design. Stick the whole thing back in the freezer.
- Call ahead to make sure the friend you are delivering it to has a big empty spot in the freezer, and add a card with these instructions: Heat oven to 500. Bake 2–3 minutes, watching it brown to "just right." Remove and let stand two minutes before cutting.

84

For someone who is going through a tough time (has lost a loved one, is facing a life-threatening illness, has had a terrible accident, or has just gotten bad news), this simple custard is a quiet offering. My mother said it best: "This custard will slide down past the lump in your throat."

Frona's Baked Custard
(Frona was Mother's best friend)

Beat slightly to mix:
    3 eggs
    1/2 cup sugar
    pinch of salt
Scald (crinkly film forms on top):
    2 cups milk
Stir together and add:
    1/3 teaspoon vanilla

Pour into 1 1/2 qt. baking dish, and set dish in pan of hot water (1" deep). Sprinkle a little nutmeg on top. Bake at 400 degrees for 30–40 minutes until inserted silver knife comes out clean. Soft center will set as it stands.

85

K eep her secrets.

When her grief is beyond words, hush! Just be there.

87

Write original poems for your friends. (This can save money on cards, and it's not only fun to get them, it's fun to write them.) No respectable person should be without a rhyming dictionary, but with or without it, poems are easy. Think you can't do it? Let me help. Choose a word that appeals to you and go through the alphabet to see what rhymes. For instance, if you chose the word "true" (friends are true, right?) the rhyming possibilities might be blue, cue, do, few, glue, hue, and so forth. You can even use the old "roses are red, violets are blue" format:

Friendship is wonderful,
Friendship is true,
You're my best friend
Tho you're straight from the zoo.

88

Eventually I hope you'll learn to write limericks. They're the most fun. We gave this one to a friend along with a gift certificate for sushi.

This gift is from friends, Wayne and Sue
Who kept wondering what they could do.
What would Dave wish?
Maybe cold, dead, raw fish!
At a restaurant that's nearly brand new.

Take an exercise class together. Go shopping for a leotard; that's good for a few laughs! After shopping, stop for dessert. Encourage each other to attend the class more than once!

90

Send letters and cards to your friend's pets. It's a fun way to keep in touch. I received a letter from my brother's cat soon after I wrote my first book. It reads in part:

Dear Aunt Sue:

... I'm impressed (a word cats hate to use) about your new status as an author. You see, I'm somewhat of a closet novelist myself. In fact, I do my best work in the closet ... the one where my litter box is. I think of it as my literary box.... In your book you talked about having a mastectomy. I can identify. I'm referring to my radical neutering! ...

Your nephew,

Max

❧ 91 ❧

When you go to the beach, bring your friends sea shells. So you have to buy them in the tacky little souvenir shop; so what? For a single friend, forget the shells, bring her the lifeguard!

92

Give a donation in her honor to her favorite charity.

For a birthday, invite the gang, rent a hearse, and go to lunch dressed in black.

If your friend is mad at her boss, offer to let the air out of his or her tires or to make a pie to throw in his or her face. Keep your fingers crossed and hope she doesn't take you up on it.

Leave a jar of bubbles on her doorstep on the first day of spring. Or for no reason at all!

96

Give your friends the benefit of the doubt.

Sometimes she may give you *the irks.*
But what about all of *your* quirks?
If you think *quid pro quo*
And forgive as you go
Putting up with is one of the perks!

Share a dessert. One plate. Two forks.

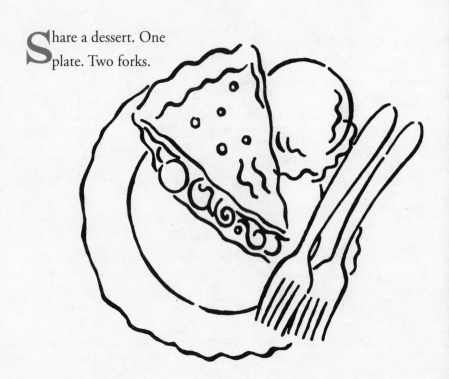

If your friend confides that she is suffering from a certain common health problem known to us all, give her a jar of prunes and a note that says,

My dear, please accept these prunes
With a prayer that by mid-afternoon
They'll quite do the trick,
You'll no longer be sick,
And no one will notice the fumes!

Arrive at your friend's house an hour before her party with your sleeves rolled up, ready to help.

✿ 100 ✿

Celebrate everything! Even a root canal! It's over, for heaven's sake!

❧ 101 ❧

Open your home and your heart to old friends and new, and do it "in honor preferring one another" as the Bible teaches us to do.